Unspoken Understanding

Ian Yearsley

Published by Ian Yearsley

Publishing partner: Paragon Publishing, Rothersthorpe

First published 2009

© Ian Yearsley 2009

ISBN 978-1-899820-62-7

Book design, layout and production management by Into Print

www.intoprint.net

Printed and bound in UK and USA by Lightning Source

Author contact:

Ian Yearsley, P.O. Box 5360, Westcliff-on-Sea, Essex, SS0 9FF

Contents

About the Author

All the poems in this collection - and many others - were written by Ian Yearsley in 2006, an incredibly productive and creative year for him.

This period of creativity was ushered in by the publication of his first poetry collection, Tears of Poignancy, a retrospective collection covering 20 years of his poetic work and featuring 30 of his poems on a range of subjects. 2006 also saw the completion and publication of his long, epic poem The Battle of Ashingdon (1016), which is written in the style of traditional Anglo-Saxon narrative battle storytelling poetry.

This current collection, Unspoken Understanding, also features 30 poems and is in many ways a more mature and much more diverse collection, with poems written in many different forms and covering a wide range of topics. Ian's traditional subjects of Love, Life and Essex provide the mainstay of the work, but there are also poems about airships, Repetitive Strain Injury (RSI, from which Ian suffers) and the environment, arguably the most important topic of the era.

Ian's poems have also been featured in poetry anthologies and Essex libraries have hosted two exhibitions of his work.

Although accomplished as a poet, Ian is best known as the author of eight history books about Essex places and is a former contributor to a range of Essex-based newspapers and magazines. He has also written on the subject of researching local history, has led local history writing workshops and has taken part in various radio documentaries about Essex places. In 2007 he took part in the Essex Book Festival, speaking on the subject of writing local history.

Ian was born and bred in Essex and has a passionate interest in his native county. He is, or has been, a member of a range of county heritage and environmental groups, such as the Essex Mills Group, the Friends of Essex Churches and the Essex Wildlife Trust. He has led or been involved in several local environmental and heritage campaigns, including one which led to the creation of the popular Cherry Orchard Jubilee Country Park on the borders of Southend and Rochford.

Apart from his best-selling books, Ian has also won several awards for his writing, including an Originality Award for his first book, The Islands of Essex, and a Twist-in-the-Tail Award for his short story, The Fungus from Outer Space. He has also been a winner in an Essex photographic competition and he co-wrote the music to an award-winning amateur film.

More information about Ian's work can be found on his website at www.ian-yearsley.com

Also By This Author

Poetry

The Battle of Ashingdon (2006)

Tears of Poignancy (2006)

Local History

Rayleigh: A History (2005)

A History of Southend (2001)

The Islands of Essex (2nd edition, 2000)

Essex Events (1999)

Hadleigh Past (1998)

Ingatestone & Fryerning: A History (1997)

Dedham, Flatford & East Bergholt: A Pictorial History (1996)

The Islands of Essex (1994)

Unspoken Understanding

We share unspoken words my love and I
And love unspoken, through our circumstances,
But I know when I look into her eyes
Or snatch some loving, quickly-glimpsed half-
glances

That she feels how I feel and in her smile
I see my joy reflected on her face
And transmit loving thoughts to her a while
To bolster sweet remembrance of the place

Where we spent time together unobserved,
Ecstatic in our union, free as birds,
Stayed separate from a world that's too demanding

And kept our special silent bond preserved.
I do not need to speak the three key words:
We have a deep unspoken understanding.

St Peter-on-the-Wall, Bradwell

How many men have sought such solitude
As I seek now in this same sacred spot?
Such stillness, silence, timelessness cannot
Leave pilgrims unaffected, unimbued

With healing feelings in this special space,
So spiritual, so calm, so awe-inspiring,
As kneeling and appealing and desiring
They seek salvation in their Saviour's place.

Outside, the sea and sky merge into one,
The chapel looms up lonely from the flat,
Like Roman sentries stood here centuries back,
A silhouette against the setting sun.

In busy, modern lives we build a home,
But peaceful isolation's our true friend.
My search for solitude is at its end:
I've finally found a place to be alone.

Coping

The thought that one day I might take a rope,
Suspend it from a branch to form a noose
And tie it tight so it will not come loose
Is all that keeps me going, helps me cope.

I've tried to find the good in dire things,
Sought positivity where there is none,
Tried trading angst for endless hours of fun,
But still I'd say that my heart seldom sings.

But ropes, exhaust fumes, airguns give me hope
That one day soon my life will reach its end.
No longer will I have to make pretend;
The thought of one day dying helps me cope.

The Clown

You share your life with acrobats and clowns
Who hide their real selves behind bright gowns,
With greasepaint and disguise your only friends,
And, self-deluding, seek uncertain ends.
You choose to live your life within these rules,
Get ridiculed, lambasted -- and by fools! --
Seek sham acceptance in a made-up world
And never let your real self be unfurled.
You jump through others' hoops, your targets gone,
Long-lost beneath disguises you've put on,
Yet all the while your search for happiness
Continues fruitless while you acquiesce,
Your own ambitions lost without a trace,
Your only smile one painted on your face.
But Time is passing and you're far away
From all the things you dream of every day.
You're nowhere near to finding what you seek:
It's time for bravery, stop being meek!
Discard those outer garments that you wear
And look inside yourself -- the answer's there!
Those clothes belong on someone else's shelf;
Don't be a clown forever, be yourself!

Brief Moments

I'm dead, I think. The signs are all around me.
On autopilot pass the zombie throng:
Automatons just going through the motions,
A world to which I never did belong.

The dullness of the daily repetition
Has deadened any sparkle in my eyes.
The loss of you has taken all the colour
And all I'm left with's fraudulence and lies.

The wood we kissed in's disappeared completely;
A motorway exists there in its stead.
Such facts as this that these days daily greet me
Provide the confirmation that I'm dead.

I never really lived, I just existed.
Though others flourished, I simply survived.
Brief moments spent with you are all I cherish,
For only when with you was I alive.

My Father

Six weeks before you died I watched you sleeping:
A peaceful, silent slumber, just your breath
Suggesting Life still had you in its keeping,
Though we both knew we'd soon encounter Death.

In soft, settee self-comfort you were dozing,
Your chest rising and falling with your breath.
And as I watched I pictured you just drifting:
You'd said that you were ready for your death.

And now these long years later I find comfort,
On days when I desire my own demise,
In picturing your peaceful silent slumber:
I know one day I'll join you in the skies.

The Field in Ramsden Heath

I like to sit by woods and hedgerows,
Soft grass underneath me,
A good view out over pleasant surroundings in
front,
The trees and hedges watching my back.

I'm neither in the wood nor out.

I like such transitional places,
Like slipways for boats
Where I stand on solid flooded concrete,
Half in the water and half out.

Is this symbolic of some wider transition?
Am I on the way to somewhere
From somewhere else?

With grass beneath and trees behind me,
I sit and think.

The Pit of Black Despair

Have you ever looked into The Pit of Black Despair
And seen the monsters lurking in the shadows there?
It's deep and dark and damp and dank and deadly down there.
You'd best avoid The Pit of Black Despair!

There is no life or light within The Pit of Black Despair.
No hope or optimism ever lingers there.
So if you hear it calling you, you need to be aware:
Resist its lure, The Pit of Black Despair!

I knew a person once who saw The Pit of Black Despair
And lingered long to look into the darkness there.
He soon climbed in to be with all the monsters in their lair,
Was lost within The Pit of Black Despair!

So if you should encounter it, The Pit of Black Despair,
Take my advice and leave before it traps you there.
The last thing in the world you want's to disappear down there.
Do not go near The Pit of Black Despair!

How do I know so much about The Pit of Black Despair?

So much about the monsters in the shadows there?

Its call is strong, I've known it long, The Pit of Black Despair.

If I go missing, you will find me there.

Canoeing

Could I canoe the River Colne with anyone,
Well I would wait 'til it was in full flood
And then fly down on it again with you,
From far Earls Colne to rolling Roman Colchester,
While watching lone lovely girls watching riverside
From river bridges, river-wide,
As we alone bridged all divides
Between us, free, and the moving sea,
Both lower than the land
But never lost or lonely here
Beneath the higher bank
Of grassy, glossy, mossy green,
All specked with sunlight,
Flecked with flowers,
Within this mid-May springtime
Midday sing-time
Sunshine scene.

We might, moreover,
Then cruise down through Colchester
And round to Mersea --
Mystery isle, still rising skyward from the magic
main --
Then add a second leg:
From there head westwards
Up the River Blackwater,
Sloshing, slithering slowly upstream

And back inland again to medieval Maldon,
Many moving miles away of ocean motion,
But reachable and unimpeachable by canoe.

So now you know that if I could
Then that's what I would do.

And yes,
With you.

Zeppelin

A giant silver bird moves in the dark.
Below it, no-one notices it's there,
Except a drunk who, wondering from a park,

Screws up his eyes and looks up from his chair.
The Zeppelin is silent, save the hum
Of high-located engines in the air.

How many of these monstrous things have come
To spread chaotic fear throughout the land?
The drunk's hair stands on end and he's struck dumb:

He cannot form the words, his shaking hand
Is partly so through drink and part through fear.
He sees it, but he cannot understand

What such a monstrous thing is doing here!
But airships changed the world in that Great War
And aerial threats would cost all countries dear
From that war on, as on our warfare wore.

RSI

[Repetitive Strain Injury]

I once was normal, just like you,
Could read and write and type and tie,
But now I sit and steam and stew
With RSI.

I cannot hold a book or pen.
My keyboard kills with every touch.
'You'll never tie tight knots again.'
Thanks very much.

I cannot text on mobile phones
Or change the channels watching Sky
Or fill out forms for cycle loans
With RSI.

I cannot use a knife or fork
Or do up buttons on my shirts.
At heavy jugs I quickly baulk:
It always hurts.

'A yuppie illness! It will heal!'
Uncaring ignorami lie,
Not knowing all the pain I feel
With RSI.

My life has changed completely now:
I cannot drive, I cannot mow,
I drink through straws and think of how
I'm always low.

I am not normal anymore
And many days I wish to die,
For nothing is worth living for
With RSI.

My Restless Spirit

Why did you have to seek so much so young?
Your foot was barely on the bottom rung
Of Life's long ladder leading to the sky
When you first asked your favourite question:
'Why?'.
Unsatisfied with elders' answers then
You set yourself the task of finding men
Who could provide the answers that you sought,
Rejecting pleasure, leisure, rest and sport
In favour of a search for who knows what?!
You seemed unable to accept your lot!
Where others relished Life, experienced joy,
You searched for answers, even as a boy.
You laughed at lesser mortals but it's true
That you're the clown -- they're happier than you!
For you cling to a fruitless, blinkered quest,
Rejecting happiness and peace and rest,
And as you grope with clumsy, clown-sized hands
It's clear you never really understand
The damage that it's doing to your head:
Just count the times you've wished that you were
dead!
Your life's been like a clown-filled, three-ring circus.
Enjoy it more. Stop looking for a purpose!

An Unspoken Telephone Conservation
(A poem for two voices)

I [He]

My heart sings when the phone rings and it's you.
Your soft voice winds its way into my head.
I feel my lust for Life start to renew

And brush aside all thoughts of being dead.
I wonder when we talk if you suspect
You help me face my past and look ahead?

Are you aware that you have this effect
And often save me from some sad demise?
By simply speaking softly you protect

Me from myself and all those childhood lies
That even at this distance cause me grief
And bring sad tears so often to my eyes.

A happy talk with you, however brief,
Instils in me a new-found self-belief.

II [She]

My firm voice searches far inside your head
For signs of the unnatural or absurd.
Do you still harbour thoughts of being dead?

I linger over every single word.
Is there a clue in anything you say?
How far have your intentions been deferred

By listening to what I've said today?
Our phone calls tell me more than you suspect,
Revealing things you'd rather not betray.

Are you aware that they have this effect
Or that I need to know you feel no grief?
My vigilance, unnoticed, goes unchecked,

Providing clues about your self-belief
And moments spent with you, however brief.

III [He-She, alternating]

My heart sings when the phone rings and it's you.
   My firm voice searches far inside your head.
I feel my lust for life start to renew.

   I'll help you face your past and look ahead.
I wonder when we talk if you suspect?
   I'd give my life to stop you being dead.

Are you aware that you have this effect?
   I look for clues about your self-belief.
On some subconscious level we connect.

   I cannot bear to see you in such grief.
Perhaps one day I'll say I feel this way.
   I love these talks with you, however brief.

You know I'm ill...
   ... although I never say.

[Both]

I cannot live without you one more day.

I Don't Like People

I don't like people
And as I lie here looking up at Fairstead's steeple,
The graveyard grass against my back,
The blue sky high above the track,
I think of people
And how they're made and understand they can be lethal.
The birds and animals are fine,
The trees and countryside all shine,
So unlike people
And as I lie here looking up at Fairstead's steeple
I'm not ashamed to tell the truth
It was the same throughout my youth:
I don't like people.
They're selfish, arrogant and cruel and can be lethal
And while they carry on this way
And say the things they always say
I won't like people.
It's why I lie here looking up at Fairstead's steeple,
The graveyard grass against my back,
The blue sky high above the track
And me alone and on attack.
I'll end with this plain simple fact:
I don't like people.

Environmental Report
(Parts I-IV)

I

No badger bothers now with Badger Close.
No meadow's ever mown in Meadow Way.
It's houses -- new, conspicuous, grandiose --
That dominate our neighbourhoods today.

No orchid blooms in pristine Orchid Drive.
No wood or farm is found in Wood Farm Way.
When builders, bricks and breezeblocks all arrive
It spells the end for hedgerows, hares and hay,

And habitats of centuries' design
Fall foul of modern methods overnight,
As planners, builders, businessmen unite
To bulldoze homes of species in decline.

So sights seen since the dawn of Earth's first day
With one fell swoop are swiftly swept away.

II

Developers don't care about lost woods,
Proceeding hastily without regret
To decimate afflicted neighbourhoods,
Indifferent if constituents are upset.

Lamenting locals lobby for reprieves
For much-loved local landscapes under threat,
But Councils and constructors, thick as thieves,
Force through threadbare proposals, targets met.

So Sprawl, fast-spreading, soon maraudes and prowls,
And looks for lives to tarnish with His touch,
For too few fret for lost farm fields and such
Or give two hoots for helpless, homeless owls.

So, on the tentacles of concrete creep
While most men, though indignant, choose to sleep.

III

Indignance, though, lies low, is little use.
It simply makes men seethe, engenders stress.
What's needed now is action, not excuse.
Stand up for England's green and pleasantness!

For while you whinge and whine and gripe and groan
About the death, destruction and distress
That moneyed men mete out on our green home
The damage does not cease and you digress.

As you in torpor gawp, as at a ghost,
Our hurt Earth, helpless, weakens with each week,
Hard-hearted harlots trample on the meek
And parasites prey on our precious host.

You know it's wrong, but ostrich-like you stand,
Your head and heart both buried in the sand.

IV

Perhaps you think there's nothing you can do?
That things have gone too far, the battle's lost?
You're wrong. There's plenty. Do it now and you
Abate a waiting later greater cost.

If not, you leave Earth's future to the few
Who counsel Councils wrongly to take heed
Of economic warnings, misconstrue
And selfish, unrepenting, feed their greed

By building buildings no-one really needs
In green and pleasant places we should keep,
Where farmers still sow seeds and blackbirds sleep;
Through them the building boundary-line proceeds.

Destruction by construction's going strong;
Would that were but the only thing that's wrong!

Snapshot

Sometimes I think my ageing Dad was right
When he looked on with sadness
At the changing world around him
And said: 'I'm OK, I'm on my way out.
It's the young I worry about.
They've got it all to come.'
And many times like him I've wished
That I was on my way out too.

And yet I should not be so keen
To wish my fleeting life away.
For other times I understand
My life is like a photograph,
A snapshot of our Earth
At one specific point in time.
And, like a camera at a wedding,
The camera of my eyes and memory
Captures and records what I encounter
In one instant -- not before, not after --
And then the instant's gone.

Will anything of true importance
Happen in my allotted years?
The advent of space travel perhaps?
The start of major global climate change?
I need to live longer than my life to know.

One thing is certain -- I am on my way out.
And it sometimes makes me sad because
There's so much more to see and understand
Than I will ever get to set my lens upon.

Love

Love blossoms, is spectacular, then dies.
It does not die a quick and painless death.
Its death is slow and lingering, its breath
Squeezed slowly out of it, its cries

Long, low and loud like screaming adults in
A row about a pointless, hapless thing,
When hate has crept up on them, when the ring
That symbolised their love's worth less than tin.

Love dies, but it should live forever and
With me it will. It will not melt like snow
At heat's first show. It will forever grow
And never die. I have it planned:

I plan to die while my love blossom's true,
So my love does not die before I do.

Poor Lambert!

Poor Lambert died when he was two years old:
He strayed too near the road just after dusk.
His former life-filled form's now just a husk;
His once-warm body's lifeless, stiff and cold.

His mum, distracted, let him leave her sight
For just one fateful second at the park.
The driver did not see him in the dark
And Lambert lost his life that star-crossed night.

He lies unburied, broken, where he fell,
All crumpled kerbside, grimed with dust and dirt,
A living thing no longer, now inert;
That he was once a fox, one cannot tell.

No human child would lie there in such strife;
We place such different values on a life.

Two Englands

There are two Englands.

The England of the countryside,
Of village life and national pride,
Of market towns and horse-drawn ploughs,
Of fields of corn and Friesian cows,
Of Sunday roasts and warming fires,
Of evening walks by timber byres,
Of family life, of fun-filled yule,
Innate respect, the walk to school,
A Fifties England, slow and free,
Its sense of real community
Still lingering in hearts and minds,
In hedgerow birds and streamside finds,
A rural world that warms the soul
And offers comfort, makes one whole.
This is the England I have known,
And yet our England's grown...

There are two Englands.

The England of the urban sprawl,
Of concrete blocks both bland and tall,
Of commerce and of global trade,
Of lies, deceit and money made,
Of charmless streets and rowdy bars,
Of noisy, air-polluting cars

Which, worshipped God-like, rule our lives,
Of thug-like kids who carry knives.
Post-Fifties England has no soul:
A characterless concrete bowl
Of anger, angst and arguments,
Materialism, indolence,
Of wanting more for doing less,
Of immigrants, red tape and stress,
An alien England I abhor
And don't want any more.

There are two Englands.

And when my generation's done,
There'll be just one.

Nudity

I made my entrance -- naked, bloody, wet --
And no-one was ashamed or thought it wrong:
With babies, what you see is what you get;
With adults, complications come along.

So somehow now it's wrong to enter in
A room of adults if you're in the nude!
We've lost touch with the evolution thing
And sex and threat are now being construed

From something that's just natural and right
By foolish, prudish twats so far removed
From human heritage that they've lost sight
Of what it means to be alive. Unmoved,

They call the police and shout: 'You must get
dressed!'.
I laugh. 'How can a cock get you so stressed?!'

Modern Poetry. Gormless writing formless writing, uninspiring, uninviting, words in assonant formations -- nations, stations, embrocations -- lacking content punctuation, words arranged without formation, words reversed (sense making never), isn't funny, isn't clever, piece of piss to criticise it, no surprise that no-one buys it! Needs return to form -- you know it! -- hallmark of a proper poet. Ditch this skirting, flirting dressage: no-one likes it, get the message!

My Country

It's easiest to start with geographics:
Off Northern Europe lie the British Isles.

The largest of the Isles is called 'Great Britain',
The second largest island is called 'Ireland'.

Great Britain is politically divided;
Its units are named 'England', 'Scotland', 'Wales'.
Except it's not as simple as it sounds,
For Wales does not exist in its own right;
It's been a part of England since the time
When it was annexed in the 1500s.
It's counted in the Kingdom of the English.
Try telling that to natives of The Valleys.

The England-Scotland border has been changed
On more than one occasion due to war.
Northumbrians must wonder who they are.

Then England/Wales and Scotland were united
By Act of Union 1707.
And thus was formed political 'Great Britain',
Its borders matching Great Britain, the Isle.

I live in England and am proudly English.
But is my country England or Great Britain?
And do I have to take account of Wales?

Historically, it's even more confused.
I'm living in the land of Ancient Britons;
The Britons live in Scotland, Ireland, Wales,
For they were dispossessed by foreign forces,
Like Angles, Saxons, Jutes and other tribes
Who came from Northern Europe to these shores.

The English, Angles once, are largely German.
I'm probably descended Anglo-Saxon,
Although it's not a thing that I can prove.

Now Ireland too's politically divided;
Two units there, so very helpf'lly named.
One is called 'Ireland', one's called 'Northern Ireland'.
The natives call them by their native names.

In 1801 GB merged with Ireland,
To be 'United Kingdom' of the two.
In 1922 this was adjusted:
The UK just included Northern Ireland.

And that's the name by which it's all now known:
The UK of GB & Northern Ireland,
With all the different countries now demoted
To what the MPs call 'constituent countries'.
They like to use vague terms like 'the Home Nations'

And like to think we all can be the same,
With typical attempts to make it all
Sound very hunky-dory to our ears.
There's been a lot of violence, so it's failed.

The 'Union Jack' or flag was then created,
A made-up symbol planned to unify.
Except, as Wales is really part of England,
That nation has no symbol on the flag.

So now I'm English and my country's England,
Or England/Wales, Great Britain or UK.

The Isle of Man is in the British Isles,
But not in Britain nor in the UK,
So why's it on the web in 'Visit Britain'?

The Channel Islands aren't in anything,
So why do they get counted in with us?

Don't start on 'overseas territories'
Or 'Crown dependencies' and all such things.

Devolved Assemblies operate in Wales,
In Scotland, Northern Ireland, but not here.
And different laws exist in different countries.
And different banks and banknotes do as well.

The British monarchy runs the UK.
The English cricket team is partly Welsh.
We're entered with Great Britain in athletics
And entered with UK in Eurovision.
My rugby team is England or Great Britain,
Depending if I'm Union or League.

The 'Flower of Scotland' is Scots' national song;
The English only have the 'National Anthem',
Although it's no specific English song,
While English football fans sing 'Rule Britannia',
A song about Great Britain not England.

And nowadays it's even more confused,
For when in Rome we do as Romans do,
While Muslims live their own lives in our land
And English people, pressured to conform,
Are British, European and confused.
Is it any wonder that there's trouble?

I blame the 'British Empire' for confusion,
With 'England'/'Britain'/'UK' interchanged.
The British Empire was an English thing,
But England, Britain, UK aren't the same;
The terms are interchanged but should not be.

Which brings me to the point where I recap...

Great Britain does not mean the British Isles.
Of all the islands, only one's called 'Ireland'
And it's a different island from GB
And yet part of it's part of the UK.

Jersey's in our country, but it's not.
And Guernsey, Sark and Herm are just the same.

The UK's cultural group's 'The British Council'.

All UK citizens are known as 'British',
Even if they don't live in Great Britain.

On census forms I have to tick a box.
I'm English, but there is no 'English' option.
I'm s'posed to say my origin's 'White British'.

My monarch is a German by descent,
But then I guess I probably am as well.

You'd think that it would be simple thing
To work out where I'm from and who I am.

When I first started out I thought my country
Was England, but I now know it's not true,
For I have looked at England from all Angles
And there is much confusion to be seen.

Until this mess is properly sorted out,
My country is the Disunited Kingdom.

Young Letters

Young letters speak of happiness and joy,
Of pleasing plans, of hopes and aspirations,
Of secret meetings of a girl and boy,
Of energy, of life, of innovations.
There is, unwritten there between their lines,
A vibrancy that's future-looking, new,
A positivity which soon inclines
The reader to the writer's point of view.
One wants to read them through, then start again,
Recalling how one felt oneself back then.

Old letters speak of sadness and regret,
Of opportunities that passed one by,
Of lost loves and of lovers never met,
Of incidents too tearful to the eye.
There is, unwritten there between their lines,
A meekness, an acceptance of one's lot,
A negativity which soon inclines
The reader to self-pity long forgot.
Young letters always raise one's spirits higher;
Old letters should be cast upon the fire.

Thax-dead

Thaxted was once a thriving town:
A cutlers' guild could quickly build
A new guildhall which would enthrall
In later times, inspire rhymes
And photographs, resound with laughs
On summer Sunday outings one
Once went upon. Those days have gone.

It once was so magnificent:
It's noble church, a falcon's perch,
Held those in awe who daily saw
Its sky-high spire rise ever higher
As cutlers' funds made moribunds
Prolong their breaths, delay their deaths
And linger on. Those days have gone.

Its commerce and its trade were great:
So much success did Heaven bless
Its busy lives with, cutlers' knives
Could fund through sales planks, bricks and nails
To build with style, still seen for miles
On Thaxted hill, a great windmill
To gaze upon. Those days have gone.

And what about those almshouses --
All trim and neat and cute and sweet
Which housed the poor, the aged or
Those most in need who could not feed
Themselves with what they little got --
The cutlers' built? There was no guilt
When they went on. Those days have gone.

What would those traders then have made
Of Thaxted now, on seeing how
The town they'd built's begun to wilt
Under the strains of aeroplanes
Above one's head from loud Stansted?
This emptying town will tumble down.
It won't be long before it's dead.

Lower Your Expectations

You've always found it difficult to cope
And always placed a lot of store by hope.
Life often gets you down, you think you fail,
But really, take a look and do not rail!
You've set such major targets for yourself
And often been frustrated when the shelf
On which your trophies were to be displayed
Remained quite empty, making you dismayed.
You've done a lot, achieved some major things!
So stop sometimes, for what tomorrow brings
Is future, you should take some time today
To celebrate your life -- you've done OK!
You've worked long hours while seeking brighter days,
Spent sleepless nights, now pause and take some praise;
Don't set your sights so high and don't forget
The many things you've done to warrant it.
Have targets yes, but don't be quite so hard
Upon yourself -- this isn't Debtors' Yard!
Enjoy the things you've done, reap their rewards,
You've had some great successes and awards!
There's one sure way raise your motivations:
Lift up your heart and lower your expectations!

Coming Out

I spent my days in secret for so long
On something I thought others thought not nice.
I consciously avoided letting on

That I indulged in such a shameful vice
And yet I wanted desperately to say
Some things about myself, but kept on ice

Those thoughts until there came that special day
When I felt finally I could come out.
I'd empathised with those who, being gay,

Live fearfully of others finding out,
But now, like them, I'm proud and want to show it!
I am myself at last and so I shout

So loud I want the whole wide world to know it!:
Accept me as I am -- I AM a poet!

St Stephen, Cold Norton

In the churchyard on the hill outside the village I
draw near
To the marble sentinel whose worn inscription
brought me here.
It's my father's father's trail I'm on for it's said we
were the same,
So I seek his final resting place and the grave that
bears my name.

Cold Norton sounds a chilling place but it isn't cold
at all
And there is no motorcycle of that name propped by
the wall.
There's the shining sun and the gleaming green of
grass around the lane
And a welcome sight of pure delight is the grave that
bears my name.

I never knew my grandad, I was six months when
he died,
But I feel I know him well enough when I look deep
down inside:
A councillor, a footballer, he found some local fame,
That army man, that father, in the grave that bears
my name.

I came to ask him questions, like 'What kind of man were you?',

'What drove you on to do the many things you chose to do?'.

I hoped he'd give me answers and confirm we were the same,

But the chiselled words stayed silent on the grave that bears my name.

My father's stories, grandad, come to life when I am here

And I feel I get to know you more each time that I appear.

I've spent such happy hours here since the first time that I came.

I'll gladly lay my bones to rest in a grave that bears my name.

I've kept it clean and clear of weeds for several decades now.

You're gone but not forgotten and I've given you my vow:

Each birthday, every Christmas, any date you care to name,

You'll find me on my knees before the grave that bears my name.

How many times I've visited! How many more to come?

I cannot tell, grandfather, but I'm proud I'm your grandson.

I'm glad I made the effort to explore along this lane

And came to know my grandad through the grave that bears my name.

My Lord, I'm sorry how I spoke you...

My Lord, I'm sorry how I spoke to you.
I did not understand when I was young.
I still don't understand completely now.

I know that if I listen I'll get through;
You've given me your word, your bond, your vow
And in return your praises I have sung,

Alerted people to the truth of you
And praised your name as I've climbed up each
rung,
Told people there's a way and shown them how.

I smell you with my nose, taste with my tongue
And put the word around that you are true.
I kneel before you, or before you bow.

The jury is no longer out or hung:
I never doubt, I know you're with me now.

Going Through My Cards

My torch beam panned the darkness of the loft
For one last time before I had to go.
The shape of one last box returned the glow;
The dusty cardboard felt all warm and soft.
What was inside? I really had to know!

I dragged the box towards the open hatch,
Where natural light would help me see inside.
I looked all round -- on top and underside --
For clues of what was in my last dispatch.
'My greetings cards' was written on the side.

I turned it round as my excitement grew,
Then opened it and cautiously peered in.
A stack of coloured cards from kith and kin
For all occasions quickly came to view.
The story of my life was held within!

'Wish I was still 18, dear,' wrote my Nan
Inside a 'Happy 18th' card I spied,
Just seven so-short years before she died.
I wished it too; the boy was now a man
And what she'd put made tears well-up inside.

The next, a gift of love for Valentine's Day.
The handwriting, disguised, proclaimed its vow,
Recalled to mind my girlfriend then and how
She'd said: 'We'll be together, come what may!'.
I wonder what on earth she's doing now?

'Congratulations on your test success!'
Proclaimed the next card, featuring a car.
'Safe driving, love,' my aunt wrote. 'You're a star!'
I always thought you'd easily pass your test!
Tear up your L-plates now and travel far!'

The next card featured twenty cartoon faces,
With names handwritten on them as a joke.
The messages inside it made me choke:
Some short, some deep and personal in places.
Lost colleagues, dormant in my mind, awoke.

A crude card next of Santa having sex
With Rudolph and a dwarf behind his sleigh.
I laughed. I knew whose this was straightaway!
'A Happy Christmas Brother!' read the text.
'Get drunk and have a really brilliant day!'

'A Happy Anniversary, you two!'
Proclaimed the next card out, sent by my Mum.
'I wish you many happy days to come
And bright and prosperous futures for you, too.'
I smiled. 'Thanks Mum, you're not the only one!'

The next card made me pause and catch my breath
As, mesmerised, I faltered in its spell.
The lilies and the sympathy spoke well
Of consolations for my father's death.
I keenly felt his loss and our farewell.

A final card with '40' on its face
(A card of sadly fairly recent date!)
Soon had me contemplating my own fate;
I mused on how Life passed at such a pace
And how my own was getting rather late.

I closed the box and sealed it with great care.
The words of long-lost friends and their regards
Might not compare with those of famous bards,
But it was sobering to read in there
The story of my life in others' cards.

Shell

Like former-hermit-crab-supporting whelks
Which, life-left, lie abandoned where they fell,
Strewn randomly with stringy seaweed silks,
Their purpose lost in flotsam-jetsam ilks,
So where they tide-line lie no-one can tell,
I serve no purpose now,
I'm just a shell.

Like empty, once-explosive, metal cases
Whose contents, battle-bound, created Hell,
Which, lifeless, litter no-man's-land in places
Or lie, trenchside, in muddy crater spaces
And like dead bodies stay still where they fell,
I serve no purpose now,
I'm just a shell.

As cockleshells piled high by shellfish shops
In Old Town Leigh-on-Sea where such shops sell
Fresh fish, shellfish, fresh crabs, crab sticks, roll
mops
And summer seafront business never stops
Discarded and ignored lie where they fell,
I serve no purpose now,
I'm just a shell.

Like prickly and now-empty conker casing
Which, child-ignored, lies ditch-side in a dell,
Not sought like stringed-up nuts that need
replacing,
Not rushed-about-for by young children's pacing,
But left to rot where they last lonely fell,
I serve no purpose now,
I'm just a shell.

I once was full of life and full of promise.
I was no fool, was full before I fell,
But now I've lost my purpose, to be honest --
I'm like a rotting tree deep in a forest --
The magic life once had has lost its spell.
I serve no purpose now:
I'm just a shell.

Lightning Source UK Ltd.
Milton Keynes UK

172691UK00001B/9/P